SELECTED DISCOURSES – THE WISDOM OF EPICTETUS

T0043366

Also available in the same series:

SELECTED DISCOURSES – THE WISDOM OF EPICTETUS
The Stoic Classic

EPICTETUS

With an Introduction by
TOM BUTLER-BOWDON

CAPSTONE
A Wiley Brand

This edition first published 2024

© 2024 John Wiley & Sons Ltd.

Registered Offices
John Wiley & Sons, Inc., 111 River Street, Hoboken, NJ 07030, USA
John Wiley & Sons Ltd, The Atrium, Southern Gate, Chichester, West Sussex, PO19 8SQ, UK

For details of our global editorial offices, customer services, and more information about Wiley products visit us at www.wiley.com.

Wiley also publishes its books in a variety of electronic formats and by print-on-demand. Some content that appears in standard print versions of this book may not be available in other formats.

Library of Congress Cataloging-in-Publication Data Is Available:

ISBN 9780857089953 (hardback)
ISBN 9780857089960 (ePub)
ISBN 9780857089977 (ePDF)

Set in 12/16pt, NewBaskervilleStd by Straive, Chennai, India.
Printed and bound by CPI Group (UK) Ltd, Croydon, CR0 4YY

C9780857089953_110324

CONTENTS

INTRODUCTION

TOM BUTLER-BOWDON

Along with Marcus Aurelius and Seneca the Younger, Epictetus makes up the trio of Stoic philosophers who are widely read today.

Whereas Marcus and Seneca were powerful and rich men of the world who sometimes struggled to live up to their Stoic ideals, Epictetus was a different beast: a professional philosopher and Stoic teacher who had been born enslaved.

Epictetus taught philosophical theory, logic, and physics at the school he founded, but most of his teachings (at least those that have come down to us in the *Enchiridion* and *Discourses*) are about character development and self-improvement. His students were trained in philosophical method, but had real-life issues and worried about their futures. Epictetus would give his formal academic lectures in the mornings, but the afternoons were reserved for more free-flowing talks about what it means to live a virtuous and successful life. His students had the same goal of mental freedom and peace of mind that you and I have today.

It may be interesting to delve into the times in which Epictetus lived, but it's his insights into human nature that are the real topic of this volume. They remain inspiring because they are based on reason, and lie outside any requirement for faith or belief.

Epictetus believed in a universe of cause and effect. Our decisions and actions have consequences that we can't change. But we also have choice or volition to act in a way that creates our futures.

He tried to show how many of the common ethical ideas of his day, such as the pursuit of power, glory, and wealth, were dead ends if they led to the giving up of one's principles and the subsequent erosion of internal peace.

Through deploying reason, we could guard our emotions and instincts and gain control over the part of our lives that was in our scope to do so. Pursuing that which was not controllable was a fool's game that could only lead to anxiety or disappointment; in short, a wasted life.

If today you hear someone saying, 'She is philosophical about it', it means that whatever event has happened to that person, it is not being allowed to affect their underlying self. Epictetus taught his students how to remain the same (literally have integrity, like a stone), regardless of externals. That is of course a huge challenge, given that it's human nature to be blown about by the winds of emotion. Yet it is really the only thing that guarantees mental freedom and peace of mind.

Epictetus never sought to have his ideas published in his lifetime, but one of his students, Arrian (Flavius Arrianus, 86–160 CE), dutifully recorded his more accessible teachings in the *Discourses* (*Diatribai*). These were published not long after Epictetus died, so we can have some confidence that they are an accurate rendering

Image: Imaginary portrait of Epictetus from the frontispiece to Edward Ivie's Latin version of the *Enchiridion* (*Epicteti Enchiridion Latinis versibus adumbratum*). Printed in Oxford in 1715.

of his thinking and his style of speaking and teaching. Xenophon helped immortalize Socrates by writing up some of his *Dialogues* and giving an account of his death. Similarly, it's only because of Arrian that we can learn from Epictetus today.

The native language of Epictetus was *Koine*, or common Greek, and Arrian's *Discourses* (of which four volumes from an original eight survive) were set down in Greek. Arrian also produced a kind of executive summary of the *Discourses* in the *Enchiridion* (Manual or Handbook). This Capstone Classics volume includes the *Enchiridion* along with selected chapters from the *Discourses* that relate to peace of mind and mental freedom.

EPICTETUS: LIFE AND INFLUENCES

Epictetus was born around 55 CE in Hierapolis (now Pamukkale in Turkey), a Greek-speaking city within the Roman Empire.

His mother was a slave, and as a result he grew up enslaved himself. At some point he moved to Rome, and worked in the household of Tiberius Claudius Epaphroditus, a freedman (former slave) who had become wealthy and who was a personal secretary to Emperor Nero.

Despite his very humble beginnings, Epictetus was brought into the proximity of power and influence. If he did not witness it first-hand, he would have been given accounts of people who had given up their integrity to win favour from the Emperor, or who forgot their ethics in order to avoid some fate like public shame, execution, bankruptcy, or exile.

Despite his status Epictetus had a fair amount of freedom, and was allowed to attend classes by Musonius Rufus, one of the great Stoic teachers of the day. That said, he did not get the comprehensive classical education that someone of his age might have received if they had noble and wealthy parents. He was largely self-taught and self-made.

Epictetus became a freedman comparatively young, sometime after the death of Nero in 68 CE. He began teaching philosophy in Rome, but was later banished (along with all philosophers, in a decree by Emperor Domitian) from the city. Epictetus established himself in Nicopolis, near the coast of present-day Western Greece but then the capital of the Roman province of Epirus Vetus.

The next few decades in his life were dominated by the school he had set up there. Wealthier Roman parents wanted their sons to have something of a classical Greek education, and Epictetus's little institution filled that gap and became successful. It was even, reputedly, visited by Emperor Hadrian, who was a Hellenophile and keen amateur philosopher. The pair were said to have enjoyed many conversations. There is a fictionalized account of them, the *Altercatio*, that was written in Latin by an unknown person in the second or third century.

Epictetus's great inspiration was Socrates: his philosophy, his life, and the way he accepted death—willingly, to preserve his principles. Other influences include Plato, Diogenes the Cynic, and of course all Stoic philosophy that came before him: Zeno, Cleanthes, and most notably Chrysippus.

In his talks, Epictetus references Chrysippus in a way similar to that of an economics student mentioning Adam Smith: dutifully. Epictetus warned his students that just reading all of Chrysippus's works—or any books for that matter—would not make them a philosopher. A Stoic philosopher was, above all, someone who *lived* Stoic teachings.

Image: Page from the *Altercatio Hadriani Augusti et Epicteti Philosophi*, a fifteenth-century illuminated manuscript. Biblioteca Nacional, Madrid.

Epictetus (according to works of art) had an unkempt appearance. He was also frugal and exacting, but readily admitted his own flaws. Using homespun analogies and stories, he had a slightly theatrical way of speaking that worked well with students. But he could be abrasive and challenging. His mission was to shake his students into awareness.

Epictetus's school demanded all his time, and as a result he did not have a family. Only after he had retired did he have some semblance of family life, adopting a son and bringing a servant woman (who may or may not have been his partner) into the household to look after them both.

Epictetus describes himself a couple of times in the *Discourses* as a 'lame old man', but it's not clear what this means. Some scholars believe he was born with a bad leg, others that he was injured by his master Epaphroditus. Others suggest it just refers to a normal infirmity like arthritis that comes with age. But Epictetus never complains; he just uses his physical condition as a means to explain his idea that physical circumstances cannot affect mental freedom. He died in Nicopolis in 135 CE.

EPICTETUS'S ETHICS

At the heart of his teaching is the distinction between what is in our control, and what is not.

We spend a lot of time dwelling on our desires, while on the other hand trying to avoid what we don't want. But much of this mental effort is a waste, Epictetus said, because only some things are actually up to us. The rest we should not worry about.

Epictetus is known for his focus on *proairesis*. A rough translation is 'will' or rational decision, involving our freedom and responsibility to act. Our will is the one thing we truly own, and so represents our true self. The body can be injured, get sick, and die, but the will is genuinely free, because it can't be affected by anything external. For Epictetus, the best example of this was Socrates, who chose to die rather than give up his principles.

Everything beyond the remit of the will should be left to Providence. Providence is not luck, rather the way that an infinite Intelligence shapes a meaningful universe. Logically, however difficult at the time, all events must be good. We use them to refine and become a truer version of ourselves.

Epictetus taught that going after external things is not only risky and difficult, but irrational. Why? You are exposing yourself to be disappointed by other people, circumstances, the winds of history, and so on. It's a recipe for anxiety and misery. Better to focus on achieving something which is genuinely in your control: how you decide to deal with the impressions and events that flood your days. By making this a matter of decision and not reaction, you can become calm and imperturbable, not blown this way and that by your emotions. What else is this but the definition of freedom?

The Stoics advocated a simple life focused on the mind, but surely it's fine to want to own a few things? Just be careful where this leads, Epictetus said. When something we 'own' is taken from us, it makes us angry or sad. It may make us want to own more of it. We can be led down an alley where we risk losing control of our emotions to something that we can never truly own anyway.

Apart from that, Epictetus noted that external things are just difficult to achieve! You'll be happier if you reduce your ambitions to improving your character. Even if you are very successful 'in the world', it is likely to affect your peace of mind; you'll either be concerned to hang on to what you have, or you want to get more to feel secure.

But can we be said to be responsible for our desires in the first place? Yes, because what we desire comes from what we believe to be 'good'. And what we think is good could be wrong or irrational. Much of what we strive for in life may be mistakenly labelled 'good' even if it does not truly serve us. A perception might be a hangover from our upbringing, or come from a sense of insecurity. By going after one (external) good, we lose another (internal) one, such as peace of mind or good judgement.

Epictetus speaks about the dangers of sucking up to powerful people. We might gain some patronage or status, but lose faith in, and respect for, ourselves. Self-respect is an achievement (one aspect of our *hegemonikon*, or the ruling principle of our soul), while the patronage may quickly disappear when the ruler falls.

It may seem a bit harsh, but Epictetus even considered one's spouse or child an 'external'. Although there may be great love between you, you cannot ultimately control their life or death. He uses a maritime analogy of the sailor going ashore and getting waylaid by the nice food he finds on land. If he gets too distracted, he'll miss the captain's call to get back to the ship (representing our true selves, or God). Attachment to family can be felt deeply, but these relationships are in the longer scheme of things ephemeral. When we are called back to the Source, only we can go.

One of the chief concepts in Stoic philosophy is living 'according to nature', and Epictetus uses the phrase often. What does it mean? As mentioned above, living according to reason means being clear on what is within our control, and what is not. It is about acting rationally in whatever circumstance arises. This is what a Stoic education tries to achieve.

If you live an orderly life, with an orderly mind, you are reflecting the rational universe that God made. We are all splinters of God, so acting in accord with nature means acting according to our rational birthright; reason is to be prized above mere instinct and emotion. Our lives can run smoothly, and be free of big torments, if we choose to live this way.

Epictetus's most famous statement is that it is not events, but our interpretation or judgement of them, that determine the state of our minds.

In Stoicism there is a crucial gap between the initial 'impression' (*phantasiai*) of an event, and the 'assent' or rational judgement (*dogmata*) we make of it. Animals and young children do not have 'assent', but act spontaneously in reaction to stimuli. The greatest thing adult humans possess is the ability to accept or discount what we are seeing and experiencing. In this space between stimulus and response, we are free. As Epictetus puts it, 'The door is always open'.

Stoic practice is about lifting the veils, so we can see reality more clearly; the way things are, not mistaken projections fuelled by emotion. Our desires and emotions colour our world, but if we can see beyond them, we can get closer to truth and live a virtuous life. Living according to reason is anything but coldness. It is fulfilment of our potential.

For Stoics, we live in an ordered universe of causes and effects, but there is still room for free will. An impression is a 'cause', but it's up to us to decide what effect that cause will have in our lives. Socrates's trial led to his execution, but he displayed imperturbability (*ataraxia*) because he alone had decided what meaning to give it.

The ability to decide the meaning of impressions and events is a great achievement. These aspects of Epictetus's ethics put together lead to happiness (*eudaimonia*) and emotional freedom (*eleutheria*).

INFLUENCE

Epictetus, although perhaps less famous today than Marcus Aurelius, had a huge impact on the Roman Emperor and philosopher. Marcus mentions Epictetus many times in the *Meditations*. Consider how remarkable this is: the head of the greatest empire the world had known admitting his intellectual and spiritual debt to a former slave.

The Roman Empire fell late in the fifth century, but the *Enchiridion* was taken up by early medieval Christian thinkers and found its way into European monasteries. The *Enchiridion* was 'Christianized' by the replacement of mentions of Socrates with St Paul, but Epictetus's theology and ethics were seen as largely complementary to Jesus's teachings.

Beyond the church, between the sixteenth and eighteenth centuries it became *de rigeur* for the educated European to have read, or at least be aware of, Epictetus. Evidence of Epictetus's teachings can also be seen in the writings of the 'father of Islamic philosophy' Al-Kindi (803–873 CE).

Among modern philosophers, Pascal mentions Epictetus in his writings, and Descartes also owed a debt to him, noting how a Stoic sense of reason could help guide life's important decisions. Politician Thomas Jefferson, diplomat and inventor Benjamin

Franklin, poet Walt Whitman, and novelist Henry James all referenced him.

In later life French philosopher Michel Foucault turned from being an archaeologist of sexuality and power to investigating what he called the 'technologies of the self'—how humans work on themselves to achieve certain goals. Epictetus's example of a life of constant refinement of self seemed to be a perfect example of this.

SOURCES

The Philosophy of Epictetus, Theodore Scaltas, Andrew S. Mason, Oxford University Press: Oxford, 2010.

Stoic Ethics: Epictetus and Happiness as Freedom, William O. Stephens, Continuum: London & New York, 2007.

Epictetus: Discourses and Selected Writings, translated and edited by Robert Dobbin, Penguin: London, 2008.

Technologies of the Self: A Seminar with Michel Foucault, University of Massachusetts Press: Chicago, 1988.

Epictetus: The Complete Works, edited and translated with introduction and notes by Robin Waterfield, University of Chicago Press: Chicago & London, 2022.

Epictetus: A Stoic and Socratic Guide to Life, A. A. Long, Clarendon Press: Oxford, 2002.

A NOTE ON THIS EDITION

The first English translation of the *Enchiridion* was James Sandford's in 1567. Elizabeth Carter (1717–1806) made the first English translation of the *Discourses*.

This Capstone edition is based on the 1916 translations of the *Enchiridion* and *Discourses* by Percy Ewing Matheson, an Oxford historian and classicist. To assist comprehension and clarity for the modern reader, I have updated some of his language and phrases.

The *Enchiridion* is printed in full here, while the second part of this edition includes selected chapters from the *Discourses*, mostly from Book 1.

ABOUT THE
AUTHOR

Tom Butler-Bowdon is the author of the bestselling 50 Classics series, which brings the ideas of important books to a wider audience. Titles include *50 Philosophy Classics*, *50 Psychology Classics*, *50 Politics Classics*, *50 Self-Help Classics*, and *50 Economics Classics*. As series editor for the Capstone Classics series, Tom has written introductions to Plato's *The Republic*, Machiavelli's *The Prince*, Adam Smith's *The Wealth of Nations*, Sun Tzu's *The Art of War*, Lao Tzu's *Tao Te Ching*, and Napoleon Hill's *Think and Grow Rich*. Tom is a graduate of the London School of Economics and the University of Sydney.

www.Butler-Bowdon.com

SELECTED DISCOURSES –
THE WISDOM OF
EPICTETUS

ENCHIRIDION

1

Some things we have the ability to control, and others we do not.

In our power are thought, reaction, the will to get, and the will to avoid. In a word, everything which is part of ourselves. Things generally not in our power are the body, property, reputation, and status. In a word, everything which does not genuinely belong to us.

Things in our power or control are by nature free, unhindered, pure. Things not in our power are weak, servile, subject to obstacles, and dependent on others.

If you think that what is naturally dependent is free, and what is naturally another's is your own, you will be miserable. You will blame gods and other people for everything. But if you think that only your own belongs to you, and that what is another's is indeed another's, no one will ever be able to compel or hinder you. You will blame none, you will accuse none, you will do nothing against your will, no one will harm you, and you will have no enemy, for no harm can touch you.

Aiming then at this high level, remember that to attain it requires more than ordinary effort. You will have to give up some things entirely, and put off others for the moment. And if you aim for status and wealth, it may be that you will fail to get them, while failing to attain those things which alone bring freedom and happiness.

Make it your study to confront every harsh situation with the words, 'You are but an impression, and not at all what you seem to be'.

Then test it by those rules that I've taught you, and first by this, the chief test of all:

> Does it fall within my control, or does it not? Is it up to me, or is it not?

If it's not in your power to determine the outcome, be ready to say that it means nothing to you.

2

Remember that the will to get promises attainment of what you want, while the will to avoid promises escape from what you want to avoid. Failing to get what you want is unfortunate, and not escaping what you wish to avoid is also miserable.

If therefore you try to avoid only what is outside of you and yet within your control, you will escape from what you don't want. But if you try to avoid disease or death or poverty, which are not in your control, you will fall into misery.

Let your will to avoid have no concern with what is not in your power. Direct it only to things in your power that seem wrong and that you can act on. But for the moment you must utterly remove desire or the will to get. Because if you desire something not in your power, you are bound to fail. Even things in your power that may be honourable to get, you may not get.

Impulse to act and not to act, these are your concern. Yet exercise them gently and without strain, and with detachment.

3

When anything is attractive or useful or an object of affection for you, remember always to say to yourself, 'What is its nature?'

If you are especially fond of a jug, admit 'I am fond of a jug'. Then you will not be disturbed if it gets broken.

If you kiss your child or your wife, say to yourself that you are kissing a mortal human being. Then if death strikes them, you will not be so shocked.

4

When you are about to take some action, remind yourself what is involved.

If you are going to bathe at the bathhouse, keep in your mind what normally happens there—water being poured and splashed, people jostling and arguing, others stealing.

You will be calmer if you say to yourself, 'I want to bathe, and I also want to keep my will in harmony with nature. I won't keep it if I lose my temper at what happens'.

Adopt this way of thinking in everything you do.

5

What disturbs our minds is not events but our judgements of events.

For instance, death is nothing dreadful, or else Socrates would have thought it so. No, the only dreadful thing about it is people's judgement that it is dreadful. And so, when we are hindered, or disturbed, or distressed, let us never lay the blame on others, but on ourselves – that is, on our own judgements.

To accuse others for one's own misfortunes is a sign of ignorance. To accuse oneself shows that one's enlightenment has begun. To accuse neither oneself nor others shows that one's enlightenment is complete.

6

Don't be elated at an excellence which is not your own.

If the horse in his pride were to say, 'I am handsome', we could just bear it. But when *you* say with pride, 'I have a handsome horse', then you are claiming the qualities of the horse as your own.

So, you ask: what *can* you call your own? The answer is: the way you deal with your impressions. When you perceive the true nature of things, then you have a right to be proud, for your pride will be in something which you genuinely own.

7

Imagine you are on a voyage, and your ship is at anchor. You disembark to get fresh water and you pick up a small shellfish or a truffle while on shore.

But you must keep your attention fixed on the ship, and keep looking towards it constantly, to see if the captain calls you.

If he does, you have to leave everything, *or* be bundled on board like livestock, with your legs tied like a sheep.

So it is in life. If you are fortunate to have a dear wife or child, they are nevertheless the same as the shellfish or the truffle. If the captain calls, run back to your ship, leaving everything, and do not look behind you. And if you are old, never go far from the ship, so that when you are called you will not fail to appear.

8

Ask not that events should happen as you will, but let your will be that events should happen as they do.

Then you shall have peace.

9

Sickness is a hindrance to the body, but not to the will, unless the will consents.

Lameness is a hindrance to the leg, but not to the will.

Say this to yourself at each event that happens, and you shall find that though it hinders something else it will not hinder you.

10

When anything happens to you, always remember to turn to yourself and ask what faculty you have to deal with it.

If you see a beautiful boy or a beautiful woman, use the impression to exercise your restraint.

If difficulties arise, look to build endurance. If you are the subject of coarse remarks or behaviour, develop patience.

If you train yourself in this habit, you will never get swept away by your impressions.

11

Never say of anything, 'I lost it', but say, 'I gave it back'.

Has your child died? He or she was given back. Has your wife died? She was given back.

Your home and possessions have been taken from you. Were these not also given back?

But you say: 'He who took it from me is wicked.'

What does it matter to you how the Giver asked it back? As long as something is given to you, take care of it— but not as your own. Treat it as passersby treat an inn.

12

If you wish to make progress, abandon reasonings of this sort: 'If I neglect my work and business I shall have nothing to live on'; 'If I do not punish my slave, he will be wicked.'

It is better to die of hunger, when you would be free from pain and free from fear, than to live in plenty and be troubled in mind. It is better for your slave to be wicked than for you to be miserable.

Begin with little things. Is your drop of oil spilt? Is your bottle of wine stolen? Say to yourself: *So what.* Say, 'This is the price paid for freedom from passion, this is the price of a quiet mind'.

Nothing can be had without a price. When you call your slave, consider that he may not be able to hear you. And even if he hears you, he may not do what you want.

Do not entrust anyone with the means to control your peace of mind.

13

If you wish to make progress, you must be content in external matters to seem a fool and a simpleton. Do not wish others to think you know anything, and if any should think you to be somebody, distrust yourself.

It is not easy to keep your will in accord with nature and at the same time keep outward things. If you attend to one you must neglect the other.

14

It is silly to want your children and your wife and your friends to live forever, because that means that you want what is not in your control to be in your control, and what is not your own to be yours.

In the same way if you want your servant to make no mistakes, you are a fool, for you want vice not to be vice but something different. But if you don't want to be disappointed in your desires, you *can* attain to that.

Exercise yourself then in what lies in your power. Your master is the person who has authority over what you wish or do not wish, to secure the one or to take away the other.

Therefore, if you wish to be free, do not wish for anything or avoid anything that depends on others. Otherwise you are bound to be a slave.

15

Behave in life as you would at a banquet.

A dish is handed round and comes to you. Put out your hand and take it politely. If it passes you by, do not stop it. It hasn't reached you yet? Don't be impatient to get it but wait till your turn comes.

Act in the same way towards children, wife, status, wealth, and one day you will be worthy to banquet with the gods.

Even when such things are offered to you in life, consider letting them pass by. Then you shall not only be in company with the gods but will share their power. In doing just this, Diogenes and Heraclitus and men like them were called divine and deserved the name.

16

When you see a person shedding tears in sorrow for a child who's gone away or died, or for loss of property, beware that you are not carried away by the impression that it is outward ills that make that person miserable.

Keep this thought by you: 'What distresses him is not the event, for that does not distress another, but his judgement of the event.'

Do not hesitate to sympathize with him so far as words go, and even to mourn with him. But don't let it affect your inner being.

17

Remember that you are an actor in a play, and the Playwright chooses the way it goes. If he wants it short, it is short. If long, it is long.

If the Playwright wants you to act a poor person you must act the part with all your powers; and the same if your part be a cripple or a magistrate or a commoner. For your business is to act the character that is given you and act it well. The choice of the cast is Another's.

18

When a raven croaks with evil omen, don't let the impression carry you away, but straightaway be clear and say:

These portents mean nothing to me; but only relate to my body or property or name, or my children or my wife. For me all omens are favourable if I decide, because whatever the issue may be, it is in my power to benefit from them.

19

You can be invincible if you never enter a contest where victory is not in your power.

When you see a person raised to honour or great power, do not let your impression carry you away. Because if the reality of good lies in what is in our power, there is no room for envy or jealousy.

Do not wish to be praetor, or prefect, or consul, but to be free. And there is only one way to freedom—to despise what is not in your power.

20

Remember that foul words or blows in themselves are no outrage to you, but your judgement that they are so.

So, when anyone makes you angry, know that it is your own thought that has angered you. Beware the need to immediately stop your impressions carrying you away.

Give yourself a little space before you react, and you will find it easier to control yourself.

21

Keep before your mind everyday death and exile and all things that seem terrible, but death most of all.

Then you will not have sad thoughts and will never desire anything too much.

22

If you set your desire on philosophy, you must at once prepare to meet with ridicule and the jeers of many who will say, 'Here he is, turned philosopher now. Where has he got these proud looks?'

Don't come over as proud, but hold fast to what seems best to you, in confidence that God has set you at this activity.

And remember that if you stay true to your path, those who first laugh at you will one day admire you. If you give way to them, you will get doubly laughed at.

23

If you get diverted to things external, and desire to get others' approval, you will know that you have lost your principles.

Be content then always to be a philosopher. If you wish to be regarded as one, *show* yourself that you are one and you will be able to achieve it.

24

Don't let thoughts such as these afflict you: 'I shall live without honour or success, and never amount to much.'

Because if lack of success or distinction is an evil, only you can involve yourself in evil any more than in shame. Is it your business to gain status or to be invited to an important event?

Certainly not.

Where then is the dishonour you talk of? How can you be 'of no account anywhere', when you should try to be successful only in those matters which are in your power, where you may achieve the highest worth?

'But I won't be able to help my friends', you say.

So, you won't be able to give them money or make them Roman citizens. Who told you that these things were in your power, and not dependent upon others? Who can give to another what is not his to give?

'If I gain wealth, everyone can share in it', you say.

If I can get such things and keep my self-respect, honour, and magnanimity, show me the way and I will do so.

But if you ask me to lose the good things that are mine, in order to win things that are not good, look how unfair and thoughtless you are. And which do you really prefer? Money, or a faithful, modest friend? Help me rather to keep these qualities, and do not expect from me actions which will make me lose them.

'But I won't be able to help my community', you say.

Again I ask: What help do you mean? You can't provide colonnades or baths. The blacksmith doesn't provide shoes, and the shoemaker doesn't provide arms. It is enough if each citizen fulfils their own function. Is it not enough that you can be a faithful and modest citizen?

'Yes.'

Well, then, you are not useless to your community.

'What place then shall I have in the city?'

17

Whatever place you can hold while keeping your character, honour, and self-respect. But if you are going to lose these qualities in trying to 'benefit' your city, what real benefit are you giving it when in the process you lose your principles?

25

Has another person been given preference to you at an event or a special dinner, or been asked to give advice instead of you?

If these things are good, you ought to be glad that the other person got them. If they are evil, do not be angry that you did not get them yourself. Remember that if you want to get what is not in your power, you cannot earn the same reward as others unless you act as they do.

A person who does not flatter the great cannot expect to get the same results as one who does. You will be unjust then and insatiable if you wish to get these privileges for nothing, without paying their price. What is the price of a lettuce? One coin perhaps. If then a person pays their coin and gets their lettuce, and you do not pay and do not get it, do not think you are defrauded. Just as they now have the lettuce, so you now have the coin you did not give.

The same principle holds good too in conduct. You were not invited to someone's grand party? The reason is that you did not give the host the price for which he sells his dinner. He sells it for compliments, to get attention. Pay the admission and go then, if it will benefit you. If you still want to go and yet not pay for the ticket, you are a fool.

But what if you do not go to the dinner at all, aren't you left with nothing?

No, you still have something: you have not praised the man you did not want to praise, and you have not had to face the rudeness and judgement of his staff when you enter his house.

26

It is in our power to discover the will of Nature by looking into those matters on which we all agree.

For instance, when another man's slave has broken the wine-cup we are very ready to say at once, 'Such things happen'. So, when your own cup is broken, you ought to behave in the same way as when your neighbour's was.

Apply the same principle to higher matters. Has another's child or wife died? No-one would say philosophically, 'Such is the lot of man'. But when one's own dies, straightaway we cry 'I am in such misery!' We should think about how we behave, given that similar losses affect others all the time.

27

As a target is not set up for the archer to miss it, so there is no intrinsic evil that exists in the world.

28

If anyone trusted your body to a stranger, you would be indignant. Yet you allow your mind to be disturbed and confused if someone attacks you. Are you not ashamed this is the case?

29

In everything you do, consider what is required in advance.

It's easy to be confident about a task at first because you have not reflected on any of the consequences. As a result, when later difficulties appear, you will give up and feel ashamed at doing so.

Do you wish to win in the Olympia games? So do I, by god; it is a fine thing. But consider the first steps to it, and the consequences, and be prepared to do the work. You must submit to discipline, eat the right foods, touch no sweets, train under compulsion, at a fixed hour, in heat and cold, drink no cold water, nor wine, except by order. You must hand yourself over completely to your trainer as you would to a physician, and then when the contest comes you must risk getting hacked, dislocating your hand, twisting your ankle, swallowing sand, getting a beating—and all this and still lose.

If you are aware of these risks, and still want to enter, then do it. But if you act without thought you will be behaving like a child, who one day plays at wrestling, another day at gladiators, another blowing the trumpet, and another play-acting on the stage. Like them you will be one day an athlete, another a gladiator, then orator, then philosopher, but nothing with all your soul. Like an ape, you imitate every sight you see, and one thing after another takes your fancy. When you undertake a thing you do it casually and half-heartedly, instead of measuring the situation and taking things seriously. It's like when some people, when they see a great philosopher like Euphrates speaking (indeed, who can speak as well as he?), suddenly wish to be philosophers themselves.

Consider first what it is you are undertaking. Then look at your own powers and see if you can bear it. Do you want to compete in the pentathlon or in wrestling? Look to your arms, your thighs, see what your loins are like. Different people are born for different tasks. Do you think that you can continue to eat and drink as you do now, indulge desire and discontent just as before? No, you must sit up late, work hard, abandon your friends and family, be looked down on by a mere slave, be ridiculed by those who meet you, get the worst of it in everything—in status, in jobs, in the courts, in every area of life. Are you willing to pay this price for peace of mind, freedom, tranquillity? If not, steer clear.

Do not be, like the children, first a philosopher, then a tax-collector, then an orator, then one of Caesar's procurators. These are not your callings. You must be yourself, good or bad; you must develop either your inner purpose, or your outward abilities. Choose between the life of a philosopher, focused on the mind, or one dealing with material things.

30

How one behaves is determined by the relationship involved. You have a father. This means you are called on to take care of him, give way to him in all things, even bear with him if he insults or hits you.

'But he is a bad father.'

Well, do you have any right to having a good father? No, only to a father.

'My brother has done wrong to me.'

Don't think about what *he's* doing, but only what *you* must do if you want to keep your integrity and retain your sense of duty. For no one can harm you without your consent; you will only be harmed when you think you are harmed. You will only discover what is proper to expect from neighbour, citizen, or praetor if you get into the habit of looking at the correct social relations implied by each role.

31

In our relationship to the gods the most important thing is this: to have right opinions about them—that they exist, and that they govern the universe well and justly.

Set yourself to obey them, and to give way to all that happens in life, following events with a free will, knowing they are guided by the highest Intelligence. Never blame the gods, nor accuse them of neglecting you.

You cannot achieve this unless you apply your conception of good and evil to those things only which are in your power, and not to those which are not in your power.

If you apply your notions of good or evil to things outside your control, then as soon as you fail to get what you want or fail to avoid what you dislike, you will be bound to blame and hate those you hold responsible. For every living creature has a natural tendency to avoid and shun what seems harmful and all that causes it, and to pursue and admire what is helpful and all that causes it.

It is not possible then for one who thinks they are harmed to take pleasure in what they think is the author of the harm, any more than to take pleasure in the harm itself. That is why a father is reviled by his son when he does not give his son a share of what the son regards as good things. Consider Polynices and Eteocles,* who became enemies by each wanting to be king. It is why the farmer, and the sailor, and the merchant, and those who lose a wife or children, revile the gods. For a person's religion is always bound up with their own personal interest. What I want to

---

* The twin sons of Oedipus.

underline is that a person who carefully watches their desires and aversions is also a pious person.

You can still make libations and sacrifices and offer first-fruits according to the custom of our fathers. But do so with purity of intent and not in a slovenly or unthinking way, and do not overspend doing it.

32

When you make use of prophecy or divination, remember to keep an open mind; you are there to learn from the oracle. The philosopher has the right frame of mind going into divination, knowing that if the event foretold is not in their control, it can be neither good nor evil.

Therefore, do not bring with you to the oracle a strong desire or aversion, and do not approach him with trembling, but with your mind made up: that the whole issue is indifferent to you and does not affect you. Whatever happens, it will be in your power to make good use of it, and no one shall stop you in this.

Confidently approach the gods as counsellors, and when the advice is given to you, remember whose advice it is, and who you will be disregarding if you disobey. Consult the oracle, as Socrates thought people should, only when the whole question or event lies in the balance. Don't go to the oracle for things that reason can help you decide on. For example, when it is your duty to risk your life with friend or country, do not ask the oracle whether you should risk your life. Because if the oracle warns you that the sacrifice means death or exile or injury to some part of your body, reason still requires that you must stand by your friend and share your country's danger. Remember the greatest prophet, Apollo, who cast out of his temple the man who did not help his friend when his friend was being attacked.

33

Lay down for yourself from the first a definite stamp and style of conduct, which you will maintain both when alone and when with others. Be silent for the most part, or, if you speak, say only what is necessary and in a few words. Talk if required, but do not talk of ordinary things—of gladiators, or horse-races, or athletes, or food or drink. These are topics that arise everywhere. Above all do not engage in gossipy talk where you blame or praise or compare others. If you can, turn the conversation to some better subject. If you find yourself in the company of strangers, be silent. Do not laugh much, nor at many things, nor without restraint.

Refuse to take oaths where possible. Or do it only as far as circumstances require.

Refuse the entertainments of strangers and the vulgar. But if occasion arises to accept them, then strain every nerve to avoid lapsing into the state of the vulgar. If the vulgar person has a stain on him, then all who associate with him must share the stain, even though they are clean in themselves.

Consume or use only so much as your bare need requires, such as food, drink, clothing, house, servants, but cut down all that tends to luxury and outward show.

Do your utmost to avoid sex before marriage, and if you indulge your passion, let it be done lawfully. But do not be offensive or censorious to those who indulge it, and do not be always bringing up your own chastity.

If someone tells you that so-and-so speaks ill of you, do not try to defend yourself, but answer: 'He does not know the rest of my faults! If he did, he would have mentioned them.'

It is not necessary for the most part to go to the public games. But if you do, show that your first concern is for yourself. Meaning, wish only to happen which does happen, and for the winners to be those who deserve to win. Then you will keep your peace of mind. Refrain entirely from applause, or ridicule, or prolonged excitement. And when you leave, do not talk much of what happened there, except so far as it tends to your improvement. For to talk about it implies that the spectacle captured you and excited your wonder.

Do not go lightly or casually to hear lectures. If you do go, maintain your gravity and dignity, and do not make yourself offensive. When you are going to meet anyone, and particularly some person of apparent eminence, keep before your mind the thought, 'What would Socrates or Zeno have done?' and you will not fail to make proper use of the occasion.

When you go to visit some great man, prepare your mind by thinking that you will not find him in, that you will be shut out, that the doors will be slammed in your face, that he will pay no attention to you. And if, in spite of all this, you still think you should go, accept what happens and never say to yourself, 'It was not worth it!' For that shows a vulgar mind and one at odds with reality.

In your conversation, avoid boasting about your acts or adventures. Others do not take the same pleasure in hearing what has happened to you as you take in recounting it.

Avoid being the comedian. It is a habit that easily slips into vulgarity, and it may well end up causing others to respect you less.

It is dangerous too to lapse into foul language. If someone else engages in it, rebuke them or make it plain to them by your silence, or a look or a frown, that you are displeased at their words.

34

When you imagine some pleasure, beware that it does not carry you away. Wait a while, and give yourself pause. Next remember two things: how long you will enjoy the pleasure, and how long you will afterwards repent and revile yourself. And set on the other side the joy and self-satisfaction you will feel if you refrain from the act. And if the opportunity does arise to do the thing, keep in mind not to be overcome by the sweetness and attraction of it. Think instead of how you will feel in knowing you resisted it.

35

When you do a thing because you have determined that it ought to be done, never avoid being seen doing it, even if the opinion of the multitude is going to condemn you. If your action is wrong, then avoid doing it altogether. If it is right, why fear those who will rebuke you wrongly?

36

The phrases 'It is day' and 'It is night' mean a great deal if taken separately, but have no meaning if combined. In the same way, to choose the larger portion at a banquet may be good for your body, but not so good in terms of maintaining social decencies. Therefore, when you are dining with another, remember not only to consider the value of what is set before you for your health, but also to maintain your self-respect before your host.

37

If you try to do something beyond your powers, you not only disgrace yourself in it; you give up the chance at a role which you *could* have filled with success.

38

Just as in walking you take care not to tread on a nail or to twist your foot, so you must take care not to harm your character. Act with this kind of caution in everything you do, and you will do well.

39

As the size of the foot determines the size and kind of shoe you need, so your body should determine all your needs. If you stick to this limit, you will know your limits. If you go beyond it, you are bound to get carried off a precipice. Just as with the shoe, if you go beyond what the foot requires, you end up wearing gold shoes, and soon purple and embroidered ones. When you go beyond what you need, there is no end to it.

40

Women from fourteen years upwards are called 'madam' by men. So, when they see that the only advantage they have is to be a wife, they become pre-occupied with their appearance and set all their hopes on marriage. We must go out of our way to make them understand that what they are really valued for is leading a life of modesty, propriety, and good taste.

41

It is a sign of a dull mind to dwell upon the cares of the body, doing lots of exercising, eating, drinking, having sex, and so on. These things are secondary. Most of your attention should be on cultivating your mind.

42

When a person says or does wrong by you, remember that they do it because they think it is right. They cannot see things as you do, and they suffer from their own deception. In the same way, if a statement of logic which is true is deemed false, it is not the statement that suffers, only the person who said it was false. If you act on this principle, you will be gentle to anyone who attacks you, saying to yourself on each occasion, 'He thought it right'.

43

Everything has two handles: one which you can use to carry, the other which you cannot. If someone wrongs you, do not take it by that handle, the handle of their wrong, because you cannot carry it by that. Rather, take the incident by the other handle—that this person is your brother or sister, who was brought up alongside you. Use this handle, and you will deal with the situation.

44

It is illogical to reason 'I am richer than you, therefore I am superior to you', or 'I am more eloquent than you, therefore I am superior to you.' It is more logical to reason, 'I am richer than you, therefore my *property* is superior to yours', and 'I am more eloquent than you, therefore *my speech* is superior to yours.' You are something more than property or speech.

45

If someone washes quickly, do not say that they wash badly, only that they wash quickly. If a person drinks a lot of wine, do not say that they drink badly, only that they drink a lot. For until you know how a person sees the world, how do you *know* that he or she acts badly? Do as I say, and you will avoid attaching the wrong meaning to what you perceive and experience.

46

On no occasion call yourself a philosopher, nor talk at large of your principles. Only *act* on your principles. For instance, at a banquet do not say how 'people' ought to eat, just eat as *you* ought. Remember that Socrates had so completely got rid of the thought of display that when people came and wanted an introduction to philosophy, he gave them one even if they were totally ignorant.

If a group discussion starts on some philosophical principle, keep silent for the most part; for you are in great danger of blurting out some undigested thought. And when someone says to you, 'You know nothing', and you do not react to it, then you are really on the right road. Sheep do not bring grass to their shepherds and show them how much they have eaten. They digest their fodder and then produce it in the form of wool and milk. Do the same yourself. Instead of displaying your philosophical knowledge to everyone, show them the *results* of the knowledge you have digested.

47

When you have adopted the simple life, do not pride yourself upon it. If you only drink water, do not say on every occasion, 'I am a water-drinker'. And if you ever want to train laboriously, keep it to yourself and do not make a show of it. Do not embrace statues.† If you are very thirsty, take a good draught of cold water but don't do it noisily.

48

The ignorant person's position and character is this: never looking to *themselves* as the provider of help or harm, but only to the external world. The philosopher's position and character is this: help and harm always come from within.

---

†As a kind of austerity, it was a practice among some philosophers to embrace cold statues when they were naked.

The signs of one who is making progress: blaming none, praising none, complaining of none, accusing none, never speaking of themselves as if they are somebody, or as if they knew anything. If anyone compliments them, they are quietly amused at the compliment. If someone blames them, they have no reaction. They go about like a convalescent, careful not to disturb their body and mind on its road to recovery, until it has its strength.

They have stopped desiring things, and avoid things only that are in their power to avoid and contrary to nature. They act with detachment. If others regard them as foolish or ignorant, they are unconcerned. In short, philosophers keep watch and guard themselves as if they were their own enemy, lying in wait for any moral failure.

49

When someone prides themselves on being able to understand and interpret the books of Chrysippus, say to yourself: 'If Chrysippus had written in a clearer way this person would have had nothing to pride themselves on.'

My aim is to understand Nature and follow her. Looking then for someone who understands her, and having heard that Chrysippus does, I come to him. But I do not understand his writings, I just seek to interpret them. So far that is nothing to be proud of. But when I have started to understand, it still remains for me to *act* on his precepts. This and this alone is a thing to be proud of. But if I am just into the power of literary exposition, then I am a grammarian instead of a philosopher, except now I'm interpreting Chrysippus in place of Homer. So, when someone says to me, 'Read me Chrysippus', and I cannot point to actions of mine which are in harmony and correspondence with his teaching, I am just embarrassed.

50

Whatever principles you have, hold fast to them as laws which it will be unholy to transgress. Don't worry about what anyone says of you, as this is beyond your own control.

51

How long will you wait to think yourself worthy of the best and live according to reason? You have received your philosophical education. Why then do you still wait for a master, so you can keep off improving yourself until he comes? You are no longer a boy, you are a full-grown man. If now you are careless and lazy and procrastinating, fixing some day in the future when you will really begin working on yourself, then whether alive or dead you will make no progress but will continue in total ignorance of truth.

Therefore, make up your mind before it is too late to live as one who is mature and proficient, and let all that seems best to you be a law that you cannot transgress. And if you encounter things that are difficult or pleasant, or glorious or inglorious, remember that the hour of struggle has come, the Olympic contest is here and you can put it off no longer. That one day and one action will determine whether the progress you have achieved is lost or maintained.

This was how Socrates attained perfection, living only according to reason in everything he did. And if you are not yet Socrates, act and live as if you were him.

52

The first and most important area of philosophy deals with the application of principles. For instance, not to lie. The second deals with proofs. For instance, *why* is it wrong to lie? The third is concerned with establishing and analysing the proofs. For instance, asking

'Why is this a proof? What is a proof, what is a consequence, what is a contradiction, what is true, what is false?" The third area is necessary because of the second, and the second because of the first. The first is the most necessary part, and that on which we must base ourselves. But most of the time we reverse the order: we occupy ourselves with the third, and make that our whole concern, and the first we completely neglect. So we lie, but are quick to come up with a *proof* that lying is wrong.

53

On every occasion we must have these thoughts at hand:

Lead me, Zeus, and lead me, Destiny,
To wherever you decree I go
I will follow free of doubt
Even if I resist and falter, I shall follow still
                                        Cleanthes

Who complies with Nature
In divine matters we count him skilled
                and wise
                        Euripides, Fragment

Well, Crito, if this be the gods' will, so be it.

Plato, *Crito*

Anytus and Meletus have power to put me
to death, but not to harm me.

Plato, *Apology*

DISCOURSES

HOW TO BE TRUE TO YOURSELF
IN EVERY SITUATION

HUMANS are rational creatures. They can put up with anything rational but can't bear what seems irrational. Physical injuries are not by nature intolerable.

'What do you mean?'

Let me explain; the Spartans bear being flogged, because they have learnt that it is in accord with reason.

'But is it not intolerable to hang oneself?'

When someone comes to the view that being hanged is rational, they go and hang themselves at once. If you look into it, you will see that nothing distresses the rational creature so much as the irrational, and at the same time they like nothing more than what is rational.

But rational and irrational mean different things to different people, just as good and evil, expedient and inexpedient, vary a lot among people. That is the chief reason why we need education, so we may learn so to adjust our preconceptions of rational and irrational to particular conditions so as to be in harmony with nature. But to decide what is rational and irrational we not only estimate the value of external things, but each one of us considers what is in keeping with their character. One person thinks it reasonable to do the lowliest of jobs. His thinking is that if he does not, he will be punished and fall into poverty; if he does it, he will avoid such a painful situation. To another person it seems intolerable to do such a lowly job. If then you ask me, 'Should I do the job or not?', I shall reply that working to obtain food is better than starving, and avoiding being beaten and poor is better than being beaten and poor. If you measure yourself in this way, go and do the job.

'But I shall be going against my true self.'

That is for you to answer, not me. Only you know yourself and your worth, and at what price you will sell yourself. Different people sell at different prices.

Consider Agrippinus who, when Florus was wondering out loud whether he should go and perform in one of Emperor Nero's shows, said 'You should go'. But when Florus asked, 'Why don't you go too?', came the reply, 'Because I do not even consider the question'. He meant that when a person once lowers themselves to think about such matters in the first place, and to value external things and focus on them, already they have forgotten their own character.

If you ask me, 'Do I prefer life or death?', I will reply 'life'. 'Pain or pleasure?', I will say 'pleasure'.

'But, if I do not act in Nero's show, I shall be beheaded.'

Go then and play your part in the show, but I will not do so. You ask me why. I answer, 'Because you count yourself to be just an ordinary thread in the tunic'. What do I mean? You think only about how you can be like other people, just as one thread in a garment does not wish to stand out from the rest. But *I* want to be the *purple*, that touch of brilliance which gives distinction and beauty to the rest of the cloak. If you say to me, 'Make yourself like everyone', I reply 'If I do that, I shall no longer be the purple'.

Priscus Helvidius too saw this, and acted on it. When Emperor Vespasian sent to him not to come into the Senate, he answered: 'You can forbid me to be a senator; but as long as I am a senator I must come in.'

'Come in then', he says, 'but you must be silent'.

'Don't ask me any question and I will be silent.'

'But I am bound to question you.'

'And I am bound to say what seems right to me.'

'But if you say it, I shall have you killed.'

'When did I tell you that I was immortal? You will do your part, and I mine. It is yours to kill, mine to die without complaining: yours to banish, mine to go into exile without protesting.'

What good, you ask, did Priscus do, being so singular? What good does the purple do to the garment? This: the purple gives the garment distinction and makes it stand out as a fine example to the rest. Another man, if an emperor like Caesar had told him not to come into the Senate, would have said: 'Thank you for sparing me.' Such a man would never have been banned in the first place, as the emperor would have known that the man would either sit silent like a cooking pot, or if he spoke would say what he knew Caesar wished and pile on more flattery besides.

The same spirit was shown by a certain athlete who was threatened with death if he did not have his genitals cut off. When his brother, who was a philosopher, came to him and said, 'Brother, what will you do? Are we to let the knife do its work and still go into the gymnasium?' he would not consent, but instead resolved to face his death. Someone asked, 'How did he die, as an athlete or as a philosopher?' Answer: he died as a man, and a man who had wrestled at Olympia and been proclaimed victor, one who had passed his days in such a place as that, not one who just works out at a gym. Another man would have consented to have even his head cut off, if he could have lived without it.

That is what I mean by keeping your character. It is very powerful if you are able to carry it into every situation.

'Go, Epictetus, have your beard shaved.'

If I am a real philosopher I shall say, 'I will not be shaved'.

'I must behead you then.'

Behead me, if it would benefit you.

Someone asked: 'How then shall each of us discover what is in line with our character?'

The bull, at the lion's approach, discovers what powers he has only when he steps forward to protect the whole herd. If the bull has a power, he naturally becomes aware of it in this moment. So each of us, who has some power, will be made aware of it. Like the bull, the person of noble nature does not become noble of a sudden; they must train through the winter, and make themselves ready, and become someone who is not easily distracted.

Of one thing beware, people: the price at which you sell your integrity. Whatever you do, do not sell yourself cheap. Consider the true greatness and heroism exhibited by Socrates and people like him.

'But if our true nature involves some amount of greatness, why doesn't everyone achieve it?'

What? Do all horses turn out winners, are all dogs good at hunting?

'What should I do then? Since I have no natural gifts, should I just give up?'

Absolutely not! Epictetus is not better than Socrates: if I am merely as good as Socrates, I will be content. Just because I will never be a Milo, does not mean I will give up exercising and sport. I am not a Croesus, and yet I will not neglect my property and finances. We should not abandon our efforts in any field just because we don't think we will win first place.

WHAT WE CAN MAKE OF THE FACT THAT WE ARE PRODUCTS OF A SUPREME BEING

IF EVERYONE could only take to heart the judgement that we are all, before anything else, children of God and that God is the Father of gods and humans, then we could never harbour a mean or ignoble thought about ourselves. If Caesar adopted you, your arrogance would be greater than anyone can bear; so, if you realize that you are a son of God, shouldn't you feel that much more elated?

We ought to be proud, but we are not. There are two elements mingled in our birth: the body which we share with the animals; and the reason and mind which we share with the gods. Humans in general are worse off through their identification with beasts, while few claim the link to the divine and blessed.

Everyone deals with each person or thing according to the opinion that they hold about them. Those few who think that they have been born to be faithful, born to be honourable, born to deal with their impressions without error, have no mean or ignoble thought about themselves. But the thoughts of most people are just the opposite to this. 'What am I? A miserable example of a human, just a bag of flesh.' But you are much more than a 'bag of flesh'. Why then do you discard the better part of you and cling to the worst?

Because of this lower identification with animals, some of us fall away and become like wolves, faithless and treacherous and mischievous; others become like lions, savage and brutal and untameable. But the greater part of us become foxes, the most godforsaken creatures in the animal world. A foul-mouthed and wicked person is no better than a fox, the meanest and most miserable of creatures. Be careful then that you do not turn out to be one of these animals. Remember who you really are, a child of God.

ON PROGRESS, OR MORAL ADVANCE

WHAT do we mean by 'progress'? It is when a person has learned from philosophy that humans desire to get what is good, and avoid what is evil. That peace and calm come to people when they get what they desire, and do not succumb to what they are trying to avoid. Moreover, that they have got rid of desires *altogether*. When they do have a desire, it is only for things within their control.

Because if you try to avoid anything beyond your will, you will learn that, for all your avoidance, you will come to grief and be unhappy. And if this is the promise that virtue makes to us—the promise to produce happiness and peace and calm—surely progress towards virtue is progress towards each of these. Whatever end the perfection of a thing leads to, it gets there via progress.

Why then, if we admit that this is the nature of virtue, do we search elsewhere for it?

What does virtue produce?

Peace of mind.

Who makes progress? Is it one who has read many books by Chrysippus? Can this be virtue—to have understood Chrysippus? If so, we must admit that progress is nothing more than understanding a lot of sayings of Chrysippus. The fact is, only virtue leads to peace of mind. And yet we are saying that it can be achieved through something else.

'That person can already read Chrysippus by himself.'

Well done! Progress indeed! So why do you mock him? Why don't you want him to see his own faults? Shouldn't you be showing him what virtue really means, so he can learn how to achieve it? You can only achieve it through work.

Where does progress lie? It lies in the region of will; that you may not fail to get what you will to get, nor fall into what you wish to avoid. It lies in avoiding error in the region of impulse: impulse to act and impulse not to act. It lies in close attention and the withholding of judgement. But if you remain afraid and anxious and seek to escape misfortune, progress is of course impossible.

Show me your progress then in all of this. Your actions remind me of when I was talking to an athlete and said, 'Show me your shoulders'. He answered, 'Look at my weights'. I don't care about your weights. I want to see the *result* of your working out.

'I have read and know Chrysippus's *On Impulse*.'

Fool, that is not what I am looking for—I want to know what impulses you have to act or not act, to know what you desire to get and what you can avoid; how you plan and design and prepare—whether in harmony with nature, or out of harmony with nature. Show me that you act in harmony with nature, and I will tell you that you are making progress; act out of harmony with nature, and I will tell you to go away and write books on such things and not just talk about them. What good will they do you? Don't you know that the whole book is worth just a few cents? Do you think that the person who expounds it is worth any more? So, I repeat: don't work in one place and expect progress in another.

Where then *is* progress found?

When you have brought your mind to think on your own will, to work out its full development, so you can bring it into perfect harmony with nature—lofty, free, unhindered, untrammelled, trustworthy, self-respecting. When you have learned that what is not in your power cannot be trustworthy nor free, indeed that you are as changeable as the winds, subservient to others who can procure or hinder such things for you. If, in a word, you can rise in the morning and guard and keep these principles, bathing like one who is trustworthy, eating like one who is self-respecting, and in every situation working to achieve their goals, just as the runner makes running their one aim and the voice-trainer their one training—this is the person who is indeed on the path of progress and who is travelling for a reason.

But if all your efforts are turned to the study of books, if on this you spend your time and money, and for this you have gone abroad, then I bid you go straight home and discover what is there. You will see that you have gone abroad for nothing. Your true work is to study to remove misery and anxiety from your life, including all sentiments like 'ah me' and 'alas for my misery', the talk of 'bad fortune' and 'misfortune'. Instead, to learn what is death, what is exile, what is imprisonment, what is the cup of hemlock, so that you may be able to say in prison, 'My dear Crito, if it pleases the gods, so be it'—and not such words as 'miserable old man that I am, is it for this I grew old?' Whose words are these? Do you think I am talking about a mean man of no reputation? Well, the same words were spoken by Priam and of Oedipus. Are they not the words of *all* kings? For what else are tragedies but a portrayal in literary form of the sufferings of people who have set their admiration on outward things? If delusion were the only means for someone to learn this lesson—the lesson that not one of the things beyond the compass of our will concerns us—then I would choose delusion if it gained me a life of undisturbed tranquillity. I leave it to you to decide what you choose.

What then *does* Chrysippus offer us?

'That you may know that these truths which lead to tranquillity and peace of mind are not false—take my books and you shall find that what gives me peace of mind is true and in harmony with nature.'

What great fortune to have this great benefactor who shows us the way! People have raised temples and altars to Triptolemus for teaching us the cultivation of the crops, yet who among you has ever set up an altar in honour of him who found the truth and brought it to light and published it—not the truth of mere living, but the truth that leads to right living? Whoever dedicated a shrine or an image for this gift, or worshipped God for it? Shall we, who offer sacrifices because the gods gave us wheat or wine, never give thanks to the gods that they produced this kind of fruit in our *minds*, which showed us the way to true happiness?

ON PROVIDENCE

EVERY single thing that comes into being in the universe gives us reason to praise Providence, as long as we have the ability to understand circumstances, and we have the spirit of gratitude.

Without these, you will fail to see the usefulness of nature's products, or if you do, will not give thanks for them. If God had created colours and, in general, all visible things, but had not created a faculty to see them, what use would they be? None at all. If, on the other hand, He had created this faculty, but had not created objects of such a nature as to fall under the faculty of vision, what use would it be? None at all. If again He had created both these, and had not created light, again there would be no use in them. Who is it then that has adapted this to that, and that to this? Who is it that has fitted the sword to the scabbard and the scabbard to the sword? Is there no one? Surely the very structure of such finished products leads us to infer that they must be the work of some craftsman, and are not constructed at random. Are we to say then that each of these products points to the craftsman, but that things visible and vision and light do not? Do not male and female and the desire of union and the power to use the organs adapted for it—do not these point to the craftsman?

If so, then the fact that the intellect is so framed that we are not merely the passive *subjects* of sensations, but select and subtract from them and add to them, and by this means construct particular objects—are not these facts sufficient to wake us up and stop us denying the craftsman? If not, then create an alternative explanation of how these things happen. How is it possible that objects so marvellously designed could have come into being by chance and at random?

Are these faculties found in humans alone? Many, yes, but many we share with irrational creatures. Do those animals also understand events and things? No—for using is one thing, and understanding is another. God needed creatures who deal with impressions: humans who both process impressions and understand them. It is enough for animals to eat and drink and rest and breed. But we, to whom God gave also the power of understanding, cannot be satisfied with these functions. Unless we act with method and order and consistently with our respective natures and constitutions, we won't achieve our goals. Constitutions are different according to different functions and ends. Therefore, one whose nature is capable only of using things, is satisfied to use them. But a creature which by nature is capable of understanding things as well as using them will never attain its end, unless it adds methods too.

What is my conclusion? God makes one animal for eating, another for service in farming, another to produce cheese, and others for different uses for which there is no requirement for abstract thinking. But God brought the human being into the world to be able to reflect on God and his works. Therefore, it is beneath our dignity to begin and to end where the irrational creatures do. We must follow where nature has intended for us: in contemplation and understanding and a way of life in harmony with nature. Do not die without understanding these things.

You travel to Olympia so that you can see the work of Phidias, and each of you thinks it a misfortune to die without visiting these sights. Yet will you have no desire to see and comprehend those things which you don't need to travel for, and which are right in front of you now? Will you not realize then who you are and to what end you are born and understand what you have been given the power to see?

'Yes, but there are unpleasant and hard things in life.'

Are there none at Olympia? Aren't you scorched with heat when you are there? Aren't you cramped for room? Isn't washing difficult? Aren't you drenched with rain? Isn't it noisy and rancorous? Yet I fancy that you balance these hardships with the magnificence of the spectacle and put up with them. In the same way, haven't you received faculties which will enable you to bear all that happens to you? Haven't you received greatness of spirit? And courage? And endurance? If you are of great spirit, why should you be worried? What will shake you or confound you or seem painful to you? Instead of using your faculties for the purposes for which you have received them, why are you instead railing against the events of fortune?

'Yes, but I have a bad cold.'

Fool! What are your hands for? Are they not to wipe your mucus away?

'But is it reasonable that there should be colds and flu in the world?'

Well, think how much better it is to wipe your nose than to complain! What do you think would have become of Heracles if there had not been a lion, as in the story, and a hydra and a stag and a boar and unjust and brutal men, whom he drove forth and cleansed the world of? What would he have done if there had been no obstacles like this? Would he just have gone to bed and slept? To begin with he would never have been a Heracles at all, if he had slumbered through his life in such ease and luxury. And if by any chance he had been Heracles, what good would he have been? What use would he have made of his arms and his might and his endurance and noble heart, if he had not been stimulated and tested by such dangers and opportunities?

'Was it his duty then to *create* such situations for himself and to seek to bring a lion, a boar, or a hydra into his country?'

That would have been madness and folly. But if they *had* come into being and were found in his world, these monsters would have helped Heracles to display his powers and test them.

The lesson then is to look to the faculties you possess, and to say, 'Zeus, send me what trials and tests you will. Because I have endowments and resources, given me by you, to bring myself honour through whatever happens.'

But instead you sit trembling for fear of what may happen, or complaining about what does happen, and then you reproach the gods. What else but impiety can result from such a deficient spirit? And yet God not only gave us these faculties, which will enable us to bear all events without being humiliated or broken down, but as befitting a good king and a true father, the Creator gave us this gift with total free will. Yet even with this free will and these powers, you refuse to use them and will not realize what gifts you have received and from whose hand. Instead, you sit there with your grievances, some of you totally refusing to recognize God, and some even through meanness of spirit reproaching or complaining about the Creator. Yet I will show you that you have the resources and abilities for a noble and courageous spirit. Show me what grounds you have for complaining and reproach.

ON AFFECTION FOR FAMILY

AN OFFICIAL came to visit Epictetus and asked for advice. Epictetus asked whether he had a wife and children. When the man replied 'Yes', Epictetus asked, 'How is it going?'

'It's miserable', he said.

What do you mean? Men do not marry and have children so that they can be miserable, but to be happy.

'Ah', the man said, 'but I am so sad *because* of my poor children. Recently when my daughter was ill and was in danger of dying, I could not bear to be near her. I fled the situation and stayed away until someone brought me news that she was well.'

Well, do you think you were right to do that?

'It was natural', the man said.

If you can convince me that it was natural, for my part I will show that everything that is natural and in accord with nature is right.

'All fathers', the man said, 'or most of us, at least, feel like I do'.

I don't deny, said Epictetus, that parents feel like this, but the real question is whether it is right. By your reasoning we must say that even tumours come into being for the good of the body, and that all error is 'natural', because most of us are prone to error. Prove to me then how your behaviour is natural.

'I can't', he said. 'Can you instead show me how it is wrong or unnatural.'

Epictetus answered: Suppose we were discussing black and white, what test should we use to distinguish between them?

'Vision', he said.

What if we were discussing things hot or cold, hard or soft, what test should we use?

'Touch.'

Well then, as we are discussing what is natural and right and the opposite, what test would you have us take?

'I don't know', he said.

Look, not everyone can know everything, but do you agree it is a loss if someone does not even know what is good and what is bad, what is natural and what is unnatural?

'Yes, that is the greatest possible loss.'

Now tell me, is every opinion that people hold, correct? For instance, the opinions of Jews and Syrians, Egyptians and Romans, on matters of food. Can all of them be right?

'How can they be?'

No, consider that if the Egyptians' views are right, the other nations' must of necessity be wrong. If the Jews' opinions are good, other people's must be bad.

'Of course.'

And where there is ignorance, there is also lack of insight and knowledge as to what is natural or true.

'Yes.'

When you have realized this, you will make this your one interest in the future, and to this alone devote your mind—to discover the means of judging what is natural and to use your criterion to distinguish each particular case as it arises.

I can help you to this extent. Do you think family affection is natural and good?

'Of course.'

And is it true that affection is natural and good, but reason not good?

'Certainly not.'

Is there a conflict then between reason and affection?

'I think not.'

If there *were* a conflict, would you say that one of the two is natural, the other must be unnatural?

'Certainly', he said.

It follows then that whenever we find reason and affection united in an action, we confidently affirm that it is right and good.

'Granted', he said.

Alright, then listen closely. You can't deny that it is unreasonable to leave your child when she is ill, even if you can't bear to see her suffering. Was it right for you, even if you love your child, to run away and leave her? Is her mother not also fond of the child?

'She is indeed.'

Should the mother then have left her too?

'Certainly not.'

What of the nurse? Is she fond of the child?

'She is', he said.

Would it have been alright for *her* to leave the child?

'By no means.'

So, should the child die in the hands of those who had no love or care for her?

'Heaven forbid!'

If you felt it reasonable for you to go away from your sick daughter because of your great affection, you cannot say it is unreasonable for others to act in a similar way. It would be absurd.

Tell me, would you have liked, if you were ill, for your relations and attendants, even your wife and children, to show their affection for you by leaving you alone and desolate?

'Absolutely not.'

If so, we are forced to the conclusion that your conduct was not that of affection.

Why *did* you act as you did then? It must have been the same sort of motive which once made a man in Rome cover his eyes when the horse he had backed was running. When the horse unexpectedly won it made him faint, so that he needed sponges to recover him. What is the motive for acting like this? Now is perhaps not the moment to define it. Suffice to say that—if what philosophers say is right—we must not look for the motive or reason somewhere outside us. It is always the same motive which causes us to do or not to do a thing, to speak or not to speak, to be elated or depressed, to flee or to pursue—the very motive which has moved you and me at this moment. You to come and sit and listen to me, and me to say what I do. What is this motive then? Surely it is nothing but this—that *we thought it right to act as we did?*

'That's it.'

And if circumstances were different, we should still have done what we thought was right and nothing else. For example, when Achilles fell into deep mourning, his reason was not the death of Patroclus—other comrades, after all, were not so affected—but his decision that it was right to mourn like this. In your case, you ran away because you thought it was right. If you had stayed, it would also have been because you thought it was right. And now you return to Rome, because you think you should; and if your mind changes, you won't go. So, in summary, it is not death or exile or pain which is the cause of our action or inaction, but our own thoughts and judgements of these events. Are you convinced of this or not?

'I am', the man said.

Then understand always that the effects of an action follow the causes. From now on, whenever you take a wrong turn, blame nothing else but the judgement which led you to do it. Try to remove wrong opinions even more than you would tumours and abscesses from your body. Your right actions will stem from right judgements, so that for instance you will no longer blame neighbours or wife or children as though they caused a bad thing to happen to you. You will know that all such judgements depend upon yourself alone and not on anything outside you.

'True', he said.

From this day forward then do not investigate or examine the nature or condition of anything—whether it be land or slaves or horses or dogs—but only your own judgements of these things.

'I hope so', said the man.

You see then that you must become a *student*—that creature we all like to laugh at—if you really wish to understand your judgements. You don't have to be a genius to know that this won't happen overnight. It is not the work of an hour or of a day.

ON CONTENTMENT

CONCERNING the gods, there are some who say that the Divine does not exist. Others say that it exists but is inactive and detached and has no thought for anything. Some say that God does exist but thinks only of great things in the heavens, and of nothing on earth. A fourth group say that God does think about earthly and human things, but only in a general way, and has no care for individuals. Finally, there is a group, which includes Odysseus and Socrates, who say:

> Wherever I move
> God sees me.
> Homer, *Iliad*, X. 279

Before anything then it is necessary to examine each of these views, to see whether they are true or not.

If there are no gods, how can it make sense to believe at all? If God does exist, but He cares about nothing, again what good will it do to believe? But if God does exist and does care, yet if there is no communication between God and humankind, what would be the point?

The intelligent person, having examined all these questions, decides to submit their mind to whatever Intelligence orders the universe, just as good citizens submit to the law of the city. The educated person approaches the matter with this question in his mind: *How can I follow God in everything, be content with divine governance, and also be free?* Because we are free if things go according to our will, and are not thwarted.

'What, is freedom the same as madness?'

No! Madness and freedom have nothing in common.

'But you say you want everything to happen as you wish, whatever that may be.'

Then you are out of your mind. Don't you know that freedom is a noble thing, and worthy of veneration? Merely to want one's random desires to be realized is not a noble thing; it comes perilously close to being the most shameful of all things. How do we act in matters of grammar? Do we write Dion's name in any way we wish? No, we are taught the correct way of writing and spelling. How is it with music? The same. It's like this in every art or science. It would not be worthwhile to know anything, if learning was up to each person's will or desire.

Can we say then that freedom is about the ability to indulge random desires? No! Education is rather about learning to frame one's will in accord with events. How do events happen? They happen as God has ordained them. God ordained summer and winter, fruitful and barren seasons, virtue and vice, and all such opposites for the sake of the harmony of the universe. He gave to each one of us a body and bodily parts and property and other humans to associate with.

Knowing this, we should not see education as being about changing the conditions of life. This is not up to us and would not be good for us either. Rather, our circumstances being as they are and as nature makes them, we should shape our mind *to* events.

Is it possible for humans to live alone? If not, can we change their nature by creating a society? Who gives us that power? We must act in a way that seems reasonable to everyone, while still staying in accord with nature.

But you are impatient and discontented. For instance, if you are alone you call it a 'wilderness'. If you are with others you describe them as plotters and robbers. You even find fault with your own parents and children and brothers and neighbours.

When you are alone you ought to call it peace and freedom and consider yourself the equal of the gods. When you are in a large gathering you should not call it a crowd or a mob or a nuisance, but a holiday and a festival, and so accept all things in a spirit of contentment.

You might ask: what punishment is there for those who do not accept things in this way? Their punishment is to be *as they are*. Are you discontented with being alone? You will feel lonely. Are you unhappy with your parents? You will be a bad son and complain about your situation. Are you unhappy with your children? You will be a bad father.

'Throw him into prison.' What do you mean by prison? You are in prison already. A person's prison is the place that they are in against their will. Conversely, Socrates was not in prison, for he chose to be there.

'What if I have a maimed leg?'

Fool, do you want to attack the universe for your one wretched leg? Why not offer it up to the universe? Joyfully yield it up to God who gave it in the first place. Are you going to be vexed and discontented with the laws of Zeus, laid down and ordained by Him with the Fates who were present at your birth and span your thread of life? Don't you know what a tiny thing you are compared with the universe? In fairness, you are not inferior to the gods, because the greatness of reason is judged not by length or height but by its judgements. Why not then align yourself with the thing in which you are equal to the gods?

'Yes, but look at the parents I have to deal with right now!'

Was it up to you, on entering life, to choose and say, 'Let this man have sex with this woman at this hour, so that I may be born?' You had no such choice. Your parents had to exist first, and who they were you had no control over. Your birth followed their existence.

As your parents are what they are, what will you do: remain miserable? Consider that if you did not know that you had the power of sight, you would be unhappy and miserable if you closed your eyes, even when beautiful colours were in front of you. In the same way, you are unhappy for not knowing that you have a high and noble spirit to face each occasion as it arises!

Things are brought to your attention, but you turn away your mind just at the very moment when you should keep it open-eyed and alert. Give thanks to the gods that they allowed you to decide what you are accountable for, and what is within your control. You are not responsible for your parents, or even for your friends, body, property, or your death or life. So, what *did* the gods make you responsible for? That which alone is in your power: how you deal with your impressions of the world and your response to events. Why then do you keep talking and complaining about things which you are not responsible for? You are just making things difficult for yourself.

HOW TO BEHAVE AROUND POWERFUL PEOPLE

IF A PERSON has some advantage, or thinks they do but do not, it is bound to go to their head—particularly if they are uneducated.

The tyrant, for instance, says, 'I have power over all people'.

Alright, you are all-powerful. So, what can you give me? Can you enable me to get what I want? How can you? Can you yourself avoid what you don't like, independent of circumstances? Are your decisions free from error? How can you claim any such power?

Tell me, on board a ship, do you put confidence in yourself or in the captain? And in a chariot, do you trust the driver to know what he's doing? What about other activities? It's the same. So, what is *your* skill or advantage?

'All people pay attention to me.'

Yes, and I pay attention to my writing board and polish it. Does that mean that it is superior to me? No, just that it does me some service, and for this reason I pay it attention. I pay attention to my horse and wash his feet so that he can take me somewhere. Don't you see that every person pays regard to themselves, and to you only as they do to their horse? But who pays regard to you as a *man*? Show me. Who wishes to become like you? Who regards you as one like Socrates to admire and follow?

'But I can have you beheaded.'

Well said. I forgot. Of course, I should worship you as if you were fever or cholera, and raise an altar to you, like the altar to Fever in Rome.

What is it then which disturbs and confounds the people? Is it the tyrant and his guards? Certainly not! It is impossible for that which is free by nature to be disturbed or hindered by anything but itself. It is a person's own judgements which disturbs them. When the tyrant says to a person, 'I will chain your leg', of course if that person values their leg they say, 'Have mercy'. But a person who values their freedom of mind and character says, 'If it seems profitable to you, chain it'.

'And it doesn't matter to them?'

No, it doesn't.

'I will show you that I am the boss!'

How can you? Zeus gave me my freedom. Or do you think that he was likely to let his own son be enslaved? You are master of my *dead* body, take it.

'But when you seek something from me, surely then you will have to pay respect?'

No, I only pay respect to myself. If you wish me to say that I will pay respect to you too, I will, but only as I pay respect to my water-pot.

This is not mere self-love. It is natural to humans, as other creatures, to do everything for their own sake. Even the sun does everything for its own sake, and in a word so does Zeus himself. But when Zeus is called 'The Rain-giver' and 'Fruit-giver' and 'Father of all people and gods', you see that he cannot win these names or do these works unless he actually does some good to the world at large. He even created the rational animal (the human) in such a way that it could achieve nothing good for itself unless it brought some service to its community. Doing something for yourself can have social benefits. You can't expect people to act in ways beyond their self-interest. You can't ignore the one principle which governs all living things—to fulfil our potential via the abilities given us.

So, where are we? When people hold wrong opinions on things beyond their control or knowledge, making judgements of good and bad, they are bound to suck up to tyrants. If only tyrants, and not their cronies too! Does a servant or slave grow wise when the Emperor puts him in charge of his personal toilet? Do we suddenly say this slave is saying smart things? I'd like to see him sacked from his toilet job, so you can see how stupid he is again. Epaphroditus had a shoemaker slave whom he sold because he was useless. Then by some chance he was bought by one of Caesar's officials and became Caesar's shoemaker. If you could have seen how Epaphroditus flattered him! 'How is my good Felicio,* how are you doing today?' If anyone asked us, 'What is your master doing?', the inevitable answer was, 'He is consulting Felicio about something'. This is the same slave who had been considered useless, who was suddenly a wise man! This is what comes of honouring anything outside one's will.

Think of a man who has been given a tribuneship. All who meet him congratulate him; one kisses his eyes, another his neck, his slaves kiss his hands. He comes into his house and finds lamps being lit. He goes up to the Capitol and offers sacrifice. But who, may I ask, ever offered such gratitude for right direction of the

---

*A common name for a slave.

will or for impulse in accordance with nature? We only seem to give thanks to the gods for what society thinks is good!

Today someone spoke to me about whether they should obtain a paid priesthood from Emperor Augustus. I told him, 'Friend, don't take it; you will spend a great deal of money on nothing'.

'But my name will be recorded in public contracts for all to see.'

Are you going to be around every time someone reads the list, proudly saying, 'That is my name'? And even if you can be there now, what about when you die?

'But my name will live on.'

Write it on a stone then and it will live on. But even then, who will remember you outside Nicopolis?

'But the position lets me wear a golden crown.'

If you desire a crown, take a crown of roses and wear that instead: you will look smarter in it.

IF YOU WISH TO BE ADMIRED

WHEN A PERSON has found their purpose in life, they do not hanker after what is beyond their reach.

What is it that you wish to have?

'I will be content if I am in accord with Nature in what I desire to get and what I wish to avoid, if I follow Nature in my impulse to act and refrain from action, both in my aims and in my implementation.'

Why are you talking in such a proud and serious way?

'I would just like that everyone should admire me, and cry aloud, 'What a great philosopher!'

Who are these people you want to be admired by? Are they not the ones you generally describe as crazy? What do you want then? To be admired by people like that?

HOW TO DEAL WITH DIFFICULTIES

DIFFICULTIES are what show your character. When a crisis meets you, remember that you are like the raw youth whom God has trained.

'Trained for what?'

So that you may win at Olympia. And that cannot be done without sweating for it. To my mind, no one's difficulties ever gave them a finer preparation for life than yours. You just have to use them, as the athlete wrestles with their opponent.

We are sending you to Rome as a spy, and no one sends a coward as a spy. If they heard a noise or saw a shadow, they would come running in confusion saying that the enemy were close. So now, if *you* come and tell us 'What's happening in Rome is terrible, death is terrible, exile is terrible, evil-speaking is terrible, poverty is terrible. Flee! The enemy is near', we shall reply: 'Get lost, and keep your prophecies to yourself. The only mistake we made was in sending someone like you as a spy.'

Diogenes, who was sent scouting before you, brought back a different report. He said, 'Death is not evil, because it is not dishonour'. He said, 'Glory is a vain noise made by madmen'. And what a message this scout brought us about pain and pleasure and poverty! 'To wear no clothes at all', he said, 'is better than any robe with purple hem'. 'To sleep on the ground without a bed', he said, 'is the softest couch'. Not only this, but he proved each point by showing his confidence, his tranquillity of mind, his freedom, and all the while being physically fit and robust. 'No enemy is near', he said, 'all is full of peace'. 'Look at me', Diogenes said, 'I am neither shot nor wounded, nor have I fled from the enemy'.

That is the right kind of scouting. You, on the other hand, come back to us and talk at random. Drop your cowardice and go back again, and take a more accurate observation.

'What should I do then?'

What do you do when you disembark from a ship? Do you take the helm and the oars with you? You take what is yours, oil-flask and wallet. If you remember what is yours, you will never claim what is another's.

The Emperor commands you, 'Lay aside your uniform'.

'Alright, I will wear one of lower rank.'

Lay aside this also.

'OK, I will wear a toga.'

Lay aside the toga.

'OK, I will take that off too.'

Even your naked body is an affront to me.

'Then take my poor body, every bit of it.'

Good, now if that is all you have, you have no reason to fear the person you are offering it to.

'But I am being cut out of an inheritance.'

What? Did you forget that none of these things were yours in the first place? In what sense do you call them 'mine'? Only as we call 'mine' the bed in an inn. If then the innkeeper dies and leaves you the beds, well and good. If he leaves them to another, that person will have them, and you will look for another. If you do not find one, you will sleep on the ground, and even then do so with good cheer, snoring the while, remembering that tragedies are always about rich men and kings and emperors. No poor man gets a part in a tragedy except as one of the chorus. In plays, kings always start with good things:

> *Crown high the halls!* and then about the third or fourth act comes—
> *O Cithaeron, why did you provide shelter to me?*[†]
> Sophocles, Oedipus the King

Poor fool, where are your crowns, where is your diadem now? Your guards won't protect you.

So, when you come near to a tyrant remember this, that you are meeting a tragic character. But it is no actor, rather Oedipus in person.

'Yes, but such a person is still blessed; look at the huge entourage which follows them.'

I too have a large company to walk with: the population of the city.

To sum up: remember that *the door is always open.* You have space to decide.

[†] The point in Sophocles' tragedy when Oedipus realizes that he began life in the uncivilized wilderness of Cithaeron.

Do not be a greater coward than children, and observe what they do. Children, when things don't go their way, say, 'I won't play any more'. When things come to a head in your own life or get too difficult, say the same: 'I will not play any more'. Be decisive. Just stop, instead of staying and complaining.

DEALING WITH DIFFICULTIES II

IF THE ABOVE is true, and if we are not silly and wrong when we say that for all people good and evil lies in the region of the will, and that everything else has no concern for us, how can we remain disturbed or fearful?

No one has authority over the things which we have control over: our principles and character. And we have no concern for things over which others have authority. So, what is left to be worried or anxious about?

'Sure, but I need specific instructions', says the student.

What instructions should I give you? Has not Zeus shown you the way? He has given you what is yours, free from hindrance and constraint. What is *not* yours He has made difficult to get. What purpose then have you brought with you into the world, and with what abilities? Guard what is your own, and do not grasp at the things of others. Your good faith is your own.

Who can take these qualities from you? Who shall prevent you from using them but yourself? When you take no interest in what is your own, you lose it.

When you have instructions and commands from Zeus such as these, what commands would you have from me? Am I greater or more trustworthy than He? Do you need any other commands if you keep those of His? Remember the main principles of philosophy. Look at how the philosophers explained them. Consider the lessons you have often heard, and the words you have spoken yourself—everything you have read, everything you have studied.

How long, then, do we need to keep these commands before breaking up the game?

As long as the game goes on.

At the Saturnalia festival it's the custom that a 'king' is chosen by lot in a game of 'Kings'. He gives orders like, '*You* drink, *you* mix the wine, *you* sing, *you* go, *you* come'. We obey, so that the game can continue.

'Now what if I ordered you to be unhappy.'

But who can *order* me to be unhappy?

Imagine we are in the play *Agamemnon and Achilles*. He who is given the part of Agamemnon says to me, 'Go to Achilles and drag away Briseis'. I go. 'Come.' I come.

Now consider hypothetical arguments. How we respond to them should guide us as to how we respond to real-life situations.

'Let us assume it is night.'

Granted.

'So, is it daytime?'

No, because I have already agreed to the assumption that it is night.

'OK, let us assume that you believe that it is night.'

Granted.

'Now, *really* believe that it is night.'

This does not make sense or follow from the argument.

It's the same in life: 'Let us assume that you have fallen into a state of poverty or misery.'

Granted.

'Are you then unfortunate?'

Yes.

'And in misery?'

Yes.

'Now, believe that what has occurred is unreserv-edly "bad".'

Again, this does not follow from the argument. Something stops me from believing it.

The question is to what extent we should submit to such instructions? Perhaps so far as is expedient; that is, so far as I am true to the game and consistent.

There are, however, some severe and sour-tempered people who say, 'I cannot dine with this fellow, and put up with his daily stories of how he fought in Mysia: "I told you, brother, how I mounted the hill: now I begin again at the siege et cetera"'. Another says, 'I would rather just enjoy the meal and hear him babble on to his heart's content'.

In a situation like this it is up to *you* to decide which you will be. Just stop being the one who is burdened and afflicted, who believes himself to be in a miserable situation. Because no-one has compelled you to be in it.

Suppose someone made the room smoke. If the smoke is moderate, you will stay. If it's really thick and noxious, you will leave. Just remember and hold fast to this: the door is always open.

An order comes: 'You can no longer live in Nicopolis.'

OK, I will not.

'Nor in Athens.'

So, I give up Athens.

'Nor in Rome.'

I give up Rome.

'Live in Gyara.‡'

OK, I move to Gyara. But it seems to me a very 'smoky room' indeed, and I leave to where no one shall stop me from living: the place that is open to every person.

Beyond the last inner tunic, which is this poor body of mine, no one has any authority over me at all. That is

---

‡ Gyara was a prison island in the Aegean.

why Demetrius said to Nero, 'You threaten me with death, but *nature* threatens you'.

If I pay regard to my poor body, I have let myself become a slave. And if I value my wretched property, I am also a slave, because I've immediately shown what controls me. Just as when the snake recoils its head and I say, 'Strike that part of him which he guards', so you may be sure that your master will trample on that part of you which you wish to protect. When you remember this, who will you flatter or fear anymore?

'Sure, but I still would like to sit where the senators sit.'

Can't you see that in this desire you are forcing yourself into a tight position in the seating arrangements?

'But how else shall I have a good view in the amphitheatre?'

Don't go to the show in the first place, and you will not be crushed! Why do you trouble yourself? Or wait a little, and when the show is done, sit down in the senators' seats and sun yourself. For remember this (and it is true universally), that it is *we* who impoverish and crush ourselves—that is to say, it is our judgements which impoverish and crush us. For instance, what does it mean to be slandered? Stand by a stone and slander it: what effect will you produce? If you yourself become like a stone, what advantage has the slanderer over you? But if the slanderer knows the weakness of the one that he slanders, then he does achieve something.

'Tear his toga off him.'

Why bring *him* (the man) into it? Take his toga. Tear that.

'I have insulted you.'

May you benefit from what you have done.

These were the principles that Socrates practised. That is why his face always wore the same expression. But *we* want to study and practise *anything* except how to remain mentally free.

'The philosophers talk in paradoxes.'

Are there no paradoxes in the other disciplines? For example, what is more paradoxical than to lance someone's eye to fix their vision? If you told someone about this practice who didn't know about medicine, wouldn't they think it ridiculous? Is it surprising then that in philosophy also, many truths seem paradoxical to those who have not studied philosophy?

ON PEACE OF MIND

CONSIDER, if you are going into court, what you want to achieve.

Because if you want to maintain your mental freedom and character and stay in tune with nature, you have all the means and ability to do so, and your trouble is over.

If you wish to remain master only over what is in your power, and if you are content with this, what more is there to worry about? Because if you own this, who can take it away from you? If you wish to be someone of honour and trust, who will stop you? If you don't want to be hindered or controlled, what person can make you will to get what is against your judgement, or stop you from avoiding things that you do not want?

Such a person may cause you troubles and even try to punish you. But they can't make you want to avoid what is being done to you. You still control your own thoughts. As long then as you retain the will to get and the will to avoid, nothing else should concern you. To follow the legal analogy, this is your opening statement, your case, your proof, your closing statement, your victory. This is your ground of boasting.

It is why Socrates, in reply to someone who urged him to prepare for his trial, said: 'Do you not think my whole life has been a preparation for this?'

What kind of preparation?

'I have maintained', Socrates said, 'what is my own'.

What do you mean?

'I never did an unjust act in my private or in my public life.'

If you wish to keep what is external to you—your paltry body, and goods, and reputation—I advise you to begin right now to make all possible preparation, and to study the character of your judge and your opponent. If you must grovel to him, grovel; if you must weep, then weep; if you must lament, then lament.

Because if you have allowed outward things to dominate your inner truth, you are a slave.

Don't be drawn this way and that, wishing to be a slave one moment and free another. Be one or the other with all your mind: free or slave; philosopher or unenlightened; a fighting spirit, or one of no spirit. Either bear attacks patiently till you die, or collapse at once.

Don't be in a position where you suffer the attacks and then still lose in the end. If such behaviour is shameful, get your own mind clear at once on what is good and what is evil, and where truth lies. 'Where truth and nature are, there is caution—but also confidence.'

If Socrates had wished to keep his outward possessions, he would not have come forward and said, 'Anytus and Meletus have power to kill me, but not to harm me'. He knew where saying this would take him. Why did he not care about the judges, in making such a provocative statement? It reminds me of my friend Heraclitus who had a court case in Rhodes about a plot of land. After demonstrating to the judges the strength of his case, he came to his concluding statement and said, 'I will not plead or grovel to you, and I do not care what your judgement will be. It is you who are on your trial, not me'. In doing so, he lost his case.

You don't have to go this far, but don't grovel either. And don't *say* you will not grovel unless, as with Socrates, you want to deliberately provoke your judges. However, why even answer the summons and go to court in the first place? If you wish to be crucified, wait and the cross will come. But if reason requires that you *should* answer the summons and do your best to persuade the judge, then do so, but always keeping true to yourself.

It is ridiculous for you to say, 'Give me advice'. What advice can I give you? Say rather, 'Enable my mind to adapt itself to the issue, whatever it may be'. For the first question is like if an illiterate person asked, 'Tell me what to write when someone asks me to say my name'. Because if I say 'Dion', and then someone else comes forward and tells him to write 'Theon', what would happen? What should he write? Who will he be now?

If you have learned how to read and write, you can prepare yourself for anything that is dictated to you. But if you have not learned, what is the good of my making a specific suggestion? When circumstances change, you need to know how to respond in that particular situation. Remember then this general principle, and you will not need my advice.

If you fix your gaze on outward things, you will be tossed up and down at the will of your masters. And who is your master? Anyone who has authority over any of those things on which you set your heart or which you wanted to avoid.

NOTES

Chapter numbers for the selected *Discourses* used in this edition:

Book 1:

Book 2: